Truth

Ruben Huys

Truth

Truth

© 2023 by Ruben Huys

1st edition - 2020 - self-published
2nd edition - 2023 - revised and expanded - self-published

rubenhuys@hotmail.com

Cover design and layout by Anna Loshchinina-Notenbaert
@nysuya_art.store

ISBN 9789464070637

Truth is a collection of poetry, writings, and quotes written by Ruben Huys.
Ruben was born in Belgium in 1991, and has been seeking for a deeper understanding of life since he was a teenager. During a period of self-reflection and introspection in 2020, he started writing down his ideas and experiences.
All of his writings reflect a sincere yearning for truth, with the aim to discover a deeper connection within himself and with other human beings.

By sharing his work, he hopes to take you on a journey of introspection, self-discovery and spiritual growth.

MISS POETRY

Dear Miss Poetry
this is me
an unborn seed
in need to be free
what is my talent?
what is my goal?
what can I do
to spark the light in my soul?
is it a job?
how can I know?
how do I turn
this life into gold?
who am I?
and how can I be?
be what I am
am what I be
have I lost faith?
have I lost hope?
I have money and work
but still I feel broke.

ROUTINE

We grow, we grow, we grow
we think, we think, we think
we reach a certain point
we sink, we sink, we sink

lost with who we are
confused within ourselves
raising all the bars
neglecting our own health

striving for success
with no wisdom inside
dying for the fame
rejecting our own light

blind to our own soul
we live like a machine
we're losing all control
when life becomes routine.

MY HEART

My heart wants me to write
my mind wants me to doubt
my heart wants to be silent
my mind wants me to shout
my heart wants me to share
my mind wants me to take
my heart wants me to love
my mind wants me to hate
my heart wants to enjoy
my mind wants to exploit
my heart wants to construct
my mind wants to destroy

the first one helps me see
the second makes me blind

I love my heart
sincerely
much more than my mind.

WORDS

Words
can be as deceiving
as our mind.

They can both
tell us exactly
what we want to hear

while hiding the truth.

CAN YOU?

"Can you feel this love?"
Asked the heart.

"No,
I can only imagine it."
Said the brain.

I WISH

I wish to see
the light that shines
in all mankind
through my own eyes
beyond the mind
behind the lies
eternal shine
through space and time
to live and laugh
to smile and find
true love and peace
in this heart of mine.

FREEDOM

You are born with the freedom of choice
to look for love
within the silence of your heart
or in a world full of noise.

SUCCESSFUL

I see a successful businessman,
yet an unsuccessful father.
I see a successful singer,
yet an unsuccessful partner.
I see a successful politician,
yet an unsuccessful friend.

I see everything and nothing
one succes neglecting the other
too caught up to the call of its voice
too ambitious to its lust and its greed.

Success is not— achieving one role or another
Success is— balancing all of our wings.

SUCCESS

Being honest with yourself
is the greatest success
you can ever achieve.

THE MESSAGE

The message and the poet
were fighting a war
the message wanted to be simple
the poet— a star
he had to be
that's what he'd been told
he had to impress
for his words to be known
he had to define
writing intricate lines
he had to outshine
composing difficult rhymes
but is this for real?
is this the truth?
is this the art?
which will inspire the youth?

he wondered one day.

HURT

Hurt is what I feel
I cannot follow my heart
sadness surrounds me
everyone is acting so smart

give up those ways
of fashion and show
surrender to truth
become one with your soul.

A MOUNTAIN

I see a mountain
so pure
desireless
without ego

it doesn't require any efforts
to convince others
from its own beauty

it just is

radiating its true nature
without any expectations
or fear
and still
everyone loves it
just because

it is.

I wish I could as well
like a mountain

just be.

DESTINATION

As I seek my destination
I sit down for contemplation
asking, wondering
what is the purpose of creation?

do I have a certain role?
what is my individual goal?
how to find those answers?
how to resolve them all?

I speak and write what's on my mind
I pour my heart out on these lines
for all I seek in these strange times
is to find joy and feel alive

but then I come back to my senses
as writing gives me glances
of what I truly represent
of what I want and who I am

and then I finally understand
my purpose
my goal
and destination

is to spread love
in this creation.

WHERE ART THOU?

Art, art, art
where art thou?

thou art the body
thou art the heart
thou art the mind
thou art the craft

thy body is beautiful
thy mind is so smart
thy craft is original
but where is thy heart?

they treat thou with lust
they treat thou with greed
they treat thou with power
they treat thou with need

art, art, art
where art thou?

INFINITE

Entertainment is temporary
Inspiration is infinite.

THE MOUNTAIN

The mountain is there
watching
as an eternal observer
greeting me with its magic

it soothes me
and awakens my purest desires

it provides me with natural wisdom
and inspiration

as if the mountain is the source of all beauty
silently waiting

until I am ready to see.

RHYME

Why would I try
to make a complex rhyme
time after time
if I can talk to you directly
line after line
I don't feel the need
to impress your intelligent mind
I feel the need
to share with you some truth
truth is simple
it is what makes us unite
it is what makes us feel bright

we don't have to impress each other with words
by showing off how smart that we are
let us use silence and love
to respect each other straight from the heart
there is no need to analyse these words
just let them be what they are
and let them be heard
let the love behind them enter your soul
enjoy this moment
then get up and go
inspire yourself
inspire another
don't wait till tomorrow
to be who you are

just be.

SIMPLE

I prefer
not to use
complicated words

because my love
for you
is simple.

SIMPLICITY

Since childhood we are made to believe that we have to impress others in order to get their attention. We think we will receive love and affection by doing so, while this artificial behaviour will only lead us further away from our true Self.
Others might consider you as simple or boring when you are not indulging in this extroverted behaviour. Even more, your silence and gravity might be confronting for them. It could make them feel uncomfortable, if they are restless inside; if they haven't found the peace yet they are looking for.
Simplicity will make you calm, confident and joyful within, while you can still be very dynamic and creative. Many great ideas and meaningful things in life have their roots in simplicity. Enjoy it.

DEAR SELF

Dear Self
please balance my words
when I speak to the masses
let only Your truth now be heard

free me from pain
free me from doubts
let the sun in my heart
shine
as it does in the clouds

enter my mind
enlighten my soul
let me surrender
to the One in control

this harsh world
full of desires
can be irresistibly tough
but the satisfaction it gives
is never enough

deep down this heart
I know
and recognise You
that Your wisdom and love
will always stay true

You are my anchor
You are my rock
wherein confusion and sadness
do finally stop

I thank You
dear Self
for being
a brother
a teacher
a mother
a friend

to You I surrender
through You I ascend.

O DEAR

"O dear earthling," said He
"How did this madness come to thee?
my eyes hurt with what I see
thine heart filled up with greed

this earth looks like a grave
thy mind is so enslaved
your toughness is not brave
why do you so behave?

I long for you to be
so beautiful and free
where you can start to see
thy own eternity

I pray for you today
thine hate may finally fade
thy lust may now decay
and love will find your way."

IMPRESS

The second I try to impress you
is the moment I lose myself.

NOTHING ELSE

I put my heart
and soul in these words

I have nothing else to give.

HOME

The mind is complex
it tells me to doubt
it tells me to fear
it tells me to shout

it leads me to anger
it leads me to hate
it makes me lose hope
it makes me lose faith

the heart is the place
where I come to rest
dissolving my sorrows
withdrawing my stress

it leads me to love
it leads me to peace
it makes me feel good
it makes me at ease

why do we struggle
to follow the heart?
because we've been taught
that we should be smart

that we should be strong
that we should be brave
that we should work hard
for acceptance and praise

but these are mistakes
this is not true
these are the lies
that linger in you

the work is within
deep in your soul
the work is in silence
to master your own

see for yourself
discover your truth
the truth in your heart
inspire the youth

they are confused
they go astray
while love is the answer
to show them the way

not from the mind
but straight from the heart
let them discover
that there lies their art

the true art of life
to be who you are
that is the work
to reach for the stars

don't look outside
but look in your own
the love of your heart
the only way home.

SPACE

If the heart gets space to breathe
love will find its ways to speak.

REPEAT

Repeat fear and fear will repeat you
repeat love and love will repeat you
one follows the other

the choice is yours.

DOUBTS

Fear is the root of those dominant doubts preventing us from opening the gates of truth. The same gates our soul is yearning to unlock in search of fresh air and freedom.
The doubts that prevent us from feeling absolutely satisfied with our Self and our surroundings, are the real barriers stopping us from walking the path we are meant to walk.

FACADE

You can put up a facade
as much as you want

but the mirror won't lie.

39

BELIEVE

To believe in yourself
is to actually do something
in what you believe.

DON'T

Don't sit and wait
because no one
will hesitate
with you.

41

GROWING

The mind expands
like a machine
the body shines
it wants to be seen
we grow older
the cup stays empty
the nectar is dry
the juice is sour
the soul is yearning

reversibility is needed
to water the seeds
to feed the roots

we grow older
like a tree
but where are the fruits?

RESURRECTION

Death—
a state of being
the heart no longer relates to the brain
misery is all I see
my soul is hurting in pain.

Resurrection, come now!
enlighten that spark in my heart!
let the bird outgrow its shell
and leave behind its premature life in the dark.

THE SOURCE

What is the source
within all of our hearts?
And what is the source
making us all feel so smart?

One is divine
which gives
and has nothing to gain.
Two is the mind
which takes
in search of fortune and fame.

Am I the one?
Or am I the two?
To balance them both
is what I should do.

The joy of our lives
lies in between.
The union of heart and mind
makes everything clean.

See with pure eyes
and feel with your soul
manifest both their powers
and you will be whole.

PRAYER

Open the path
to freedom and truth
open our minds
for the absolute fruit
the fruits of our life
to be sown in our soul
the fruits of our life
to become and evolve
to become who we are
free from the pain
to live from the heart
not just the brain

please Lord
great power of Self
come now!
bestow all your grace
let us surrender
all that is fake

You are the light
You are the love
the love in our hearts
not just above.

TODAY

Today is the day
where love will conquer
fear can no longer bind me to its lies
freedom is calling
I have to answer
answer the voice which is calling inside
truth will be told
and I will be new
today is the day
I surrender to You.

YOU

You are the light
You are the way
You are the night
You are the day
You are the heart
You are the mind
You are the one
beyond limits and time
to You belongs all
all comes from You
to You I surrender
that's all I can do
show me the path
show me the way
to turn the darkness of night
into the brightness of day.

THE HEART

If darkness is death
please show me the light
if sadness surrounds me
please show me the light
if jealousy attacks me
please show me the light
if anger destroys me
please show me the light

let the light of my heart
dissolve hatred and fear
let the light of my heart
be very near

sometimes it comes
sometimes it goes
the light of my heart
the light of my soul

the love it provides
is all that I need
the love it provides
is all I can give

no words that I speak
can heal all the wounds
no words that I speak
can reveal all the truth

only the heart
and the light that it gives
only the heart
is in what I believe.

REVEAL

I call out the Source
from where I done came
I call out its voice
to spit fire and flames
reveal us Your Self
reveal us Your truth
whatever was old
should now become new
open Your doors
for us to come in
Your gates are unlocked
but where to begin
we are so lost
while we are searching
we are looking outside
while You are within.

CHANGE

The rules have changed
I'm set free
fear and doubt
now cease to be
a slave of thought
is what I was
a warrior of heart
is what I am

transformation is the key
for this seed to grow
and become a tree

fruits shall come
from this mysterious fight
fruits shall come
as it is the law of life.

GIVING

Life has taught me
that the joy of giving
is all I can take
from this world.

JUST HERE

I'm just here
all by myself
the chaos in my head
has now come to rest
there is nothing to worry about
I have nothing to fear

I am exactly
where I want to be
just here
all by myself
with my heart
and my pen

and now
you are with me.

WHO ARE YOU?

The message had to come
it could no longer wait to reveal itself
it requires courage and faith
its voice speaks clearly:
be who you are

who are you?
have you ever questioned yourself?

the message is here
it's calling your heart
listen to it:

part ways with false ideas and thoughts
worldly worries and doubts
identity is merely an illusion
now is the time to break out

eternity is within
there lies the most powerful force
providing all the answers you need
unlocking all your wonderful doors.

CLARITY

Ask for clarity in your life
sincerely
honestly
and clarity will come to you.

It's that simple
but we are taught
to make things complicated.

Have faith.

DO YOU?

Do you really care about peace in this world?
or do you only care about diamonds and pearls?
do you really care about love and respect?
or do you only care about money and sex?

well

one path might steer you to darkness
the other will show you the light
but you have the freedom to choose
which direction you follow in life.

IF ONLY

I would reward you
with compliments
praise
prosperity and wealth

if only it could help
for you to love yourself.

LAWS

To change something outside, we have to first change within. These are the laws that life has bestowed upon us. No one else will do it for us. No one else will teach us how to love.
We have to love ourselves first, before we can love another. We have to change ourselves first, before anything else can change. These are the laws that life has bestowed upon us. Accept them; if you care.

CLEANSE

These words flow like a stream of water
undisturbed
filling every space
they nourish and rinse
drink from its source
let them cleanse.

QUOTE

The beauty of a good quote
is when it touches your heart sincerely
while you get the feeling
you could have written it
yourself.

THE BARBER

I sat at the barber and wondered
watching the young man in the chair
getting his hair done
I asked myself
does it make him happy?
does it make him stronger?
the lines on the sides were so specific
every detail was in place
I saw him proudly looking in the mirror
although he seemed disturbed
he seemed so far away
away from himself
not knowing who he actually was
nor having a clue about his purpose in life
everything depending on his hair
his hair— was his identity
while sitting on that chair.

MIRROR

The man in the mirror
is staring straight into my soul
he knows exactly who I am
he wants to reveal it directly to my face
still, he remains silent
quietly reflecting
the picture portrayed in front of him.

It is not his duty to correct me
neither to engage
he's just there
watching
judgeless
as he always was
and will.

Regardless of what I do
despite how much I change
the man in the mirror
is always the same.

THAT DAY

That day
when your public image
and your true personality
finally become one

you will feel complete.

CONFIDENCE

Confidence is a subtle feeling inside. It doesn't have to be proven to the outside world. It is a connection with yourself that you should strongly value and appreciate. When you are confident within, it will naturally emit to your environment, without you having to make any effort. The more you try to prove yourself, the more your ego will take charge. Ego is not a sign of confidence. It is often an expression of underlying insecurity and doubt.

No one else can really tell you who you are. No one can fully help you to become yourself.
They can only be an inspiration to enlighten that source of wisdom deep within yourself, so that eventually you can discover everything you are on your own.

INSPIRE

All I want
is to inspire you
so you can inspire yourself
and others
the circle of life
inspire each other.

SINCERITY

These motivational quotes and poems will only relieve you from your worries and problems for a short amount of time, before they come back haunting you. If you truly want to motivate yourself and change something about your life, then start with looking into the mirror every day. Dive deep into your soul and ask yourself whether you are being honest and sincere about your own thoughts and actions; about every single one of them. Whether you are being who you truly are, or if you are deceiving yourself with your own ego and justifications. The answers and solutions that you will receive from that type of introspection will help you a thousand times more, than reading a thousand quotes.

HEY YOU

Hey you
yes you
do you not see?

that the blind lead the blind
that we are not free?

that we are enslaved
by their opinions and thoughts
by their wicked ideas
that our love can be bought

that love is for sale
without question of heart
but does a painting without love
breathe the beauty of art?

the love they sell us is cheap
and feels awfully dark
like a man without soul
yet incredibly smart

what is their objective?
what do you say?
when they sell you this nonsense
each and every day

do you resist?
do you stand strong?
do you know the purpose of love?
and where it belongs?

it is not on the streets
nor in any old book
it lingers deep in our hearts
that is where we should look

now,
do you believe
in these words I just said?

go,
believe in yourself
and choose life over death.

TRAVELLED

I travelled all corners of the world
to discover that home
exists deep in my heart.

Now I'm free.

COUNTRIES

Countries are an illusion
man made maps
with borders and regulations
intentionally dividing
and creating confusion
binding us to patriotic ideas and thoughts

thoughts about what?
nothing

the whole world is my country
and love is my home.

WAR

War is everywhere
but it starts in the mind
war is normal
when the blind lead the blind
ignorance is bliss
is what they make us believe
ignorance is death
is what I know
war is a weapon
to keep us in place
war is their strength
to make us afraid
how can this fear
shatter our souls
how can this fear
destroy the whole globe
fear is a tool
to make us a fool
fear is the worst enemy of ourselves
they feed us with it
everywhere that we go
they feed us with fear
to forget about soul
to forget about love
to forget about joy
to forget about truth
to forget about youth
we blame the whole world
but fear is the root

our fear
the fear within you.

LET US FEEL

There is a connection between
human beings which we cannot fathom
there is a connection between
human beings which we don't want to hear
it is too simple for our intelligent brains to accept
we want scientific proof before we acknowledge it
we all know it's there
we all know it's here
it is just waiting for us
to be finally set free
the more you think about it
the more it hides
the more you need proof
the less you will feel
to feel is to know
and to know is to feel

let us feel.

EXPERIENCE

There is a huge gap
between believing in something
and knowing through experience.

DESTINY

When your attention unites with your deepest
desire, everything is possible. If you truly believe in
what you feel, because it makes your whole being
at ease, then go for it. You have to manifest your
desire out there in the world by taking action.
When your attention is pure and you really want
something, all the natural elements will start
working together to make it happen. All the stars
will align and start shining altogether, so that you
can manifest your destiny. Just believe in what you
truly want; and follow it.

PERFECTIONIST

Being a perfectionist
is being able to let go.
To perfectly balance
between intention and desire.
To see the beauty of love
in the work itself.

Being a perfectionist
is being able to work hard.
Hard enough
until your soul is satisfied.

Working with love
gives satisfaction.

Everything else doesn't.

That's perfect.

NECTAR

No one else can really make you feel bad.
That is only a perception you have about
life. Only you can make you feel bad
about yourself and about how others
project their behaviour on you. You can
only be influenced by a storm, if it is
storming inside.
Be like a tree. Stand firm and watch. Trees
never feel insulted, not even when you
cut them. They will still provide nectar
for their fruits.
Be that tree, and always provide nectar for
your own soul. Because you're worth it;
that's truth.

SURRENDER

People are afraid of change
because they lack gravity.
We have been trained
to hold on to anything we consider as safe.
Mental barriers
the modern day slave.
The fear to lose control is destroying our joy;
the fear to accept the unknown
and to be spontaneous is killing our soul.
The soul is free;
an eternal being of love, light and wonder.
It can only be fed through following your intuition
and courage.
In return
the Soul of Life will support you.

Everything will fall in place
every time
every moment
once you surrender to truth.

OCEAN

There is a light that shines
and combines
all forces of nature
to rise above the mind
it shoots out like a star
the essence
revealing us who we are
the light is within
the road is rocky
the passage is narrow
but the gates are open

follow the path
follow your heart
and discover your ocean.

I MEAN THIS

If words could give you joy
I would write them for you.

RISE UP

This is for the soul searchers
the freedom seekers
the inspired youth
and true believers

this is for those who know
but cannot fully reach
this is for those who struggle
to practice the preach

don't feel ashamed
don't give up on your goals
for we all make mistakes
and lose sight of our own

rise up
gather your strength
follow your heart
try to ascend

open your eyes
for wisdom and truth
this is the best I can give
now it's all up to you!

LET IT SPEAK

When things don't go your way, don't give up.
Life is trying to tell you something. It wants to
teach you a lesson. When you feel caught up,
and you don't know what to do, it means there
is friction between your true Self and your
mental expectations. Like a clash between your
ego and your true nature. Listen to that voice
deep within; the one that clarifies; the one that
nourishes your heart. Let it speak clearly. It will
give answers. It will support you. Listen
sincerely.

THE BALANCE

The balance of life
lies between the thought and its art
the balance of life
lies between the mind and the heart
the balance of life
can be found within you and in me
the balance of life
is mere simplicity
it is the easiest way to be free

just be.

FREQUENCY

The frequency
the wave of the wind
thoughts no longer disturb what I see

the frequency
the inner beauty
of all living things around me

the frequency
the sound of the bird
amidst all of the noise in the tree

the frequency
the silence of mind
when the voice of the heart sets me free.

WHISPER

Good deeds are the silent whispers
of those who don't feel the need to speak.

HOW DO YOU FEEL?

What can I write to you today?
Is everything alright? Are you okay?
How do you feel?
Is what I truly like to know.
Are you enjoying your life?
Or are you losing control?
Be free
to share what you think
life flies by
either you float, or you sink.
But have you found peace?
And have you felt love?
Or are you too busy
to find the above?
There is a path
there is a way
for all of those worries
to now go away;
let's come together
enjoy and sing
the voice of our hearts
heal every thing;
let it strike hard
and deep in your soul
surrender to it
and give up control.

LOVE

The true beauty of love
resides deep in our heart
as an expression of Self
a reflection of God
transformed into art.

EYES

Your eyes
move everywhere
while your soul
doesn't get a chance
to see.

STUDY

I studied myself
over and over again
relentlessly.

I studied life
by watching it
I used to fight with it
now it's my best friend.

CONFRONTATION

To truly love yourself, you have to be willing to confront yourself. You have to be able to look into the mirror and face your own misidentifications and problems.
If you really want to grow as a person, you have to work hard to change yourself. You have to find the right balance between being disciplined and being relaxed. Don't force yourself, don't become a dry personality, but be open for reflection and change. On the other hand, don't be too loose on yourself, don't accept everything as it is, because you are meant to face yourself and grow towards a beautiful personality.
We can only grow by making mistakes, but we have to be able to see them and correct them if necessary. Be very honest and clear with yourself, and life will become very honest and clear with you. Life will become your best friend; because it will feel that you take it seriously, that you respect it. And it will respect you.

THE DIFFERENCE

There is a big difference between accepting yourself and justifying yourself. They are two opposites.

Accepting yourself means understanding your current state of being, while always trying to find opportunities to improve and evolve.

Justifying yourself means being ignorant to your own responsibilities and shortcomings, while blaming your environment or your emotions without having the courage to overcome them.

MISSION

Truth is my weapon
Love is my mission.

I WANT TO BE RICH

I want to be rich
while writing these poems
I want to be rich
while touching your soul
I want to be rich
while creating pure art
I want to be rich
while touching your heart
But what is this richness?
And what are its means?
Does it mean money?
Does it mean love?
Does it mean recognition?
Does it mean respect?
Or is it a combination
of all of these things?
Not one or the other
not any extreme
just a beautiful balance
for us human beings.

I want to be rich.

MONEY

We are so focused on getting money in life, that it makes us lose a lot of our creativity, spontaneity and joy. Many things we pursue are dependent on whether it will provide us with money or not. This can drain all our energy and prevent us from discovering our innate desire and talents in the first place.
The fear of running out of money is so deeply rooted in our ways of thinking, that we might miss real opportunities opening up in front of us. We might miss the chance of finding creative ways to manifest our true passion and potential, wherein money could become a natural byproduct of those actions.

THE BRIDGE

I stood alone upon the bridge
gazing down at this mysterious world
watching
a majestic view
the chaos was tremendous
the narrative nothing new
every day the same drama
every day the same game
people
looking for something
but with their own behaviour
they feel no shame
change
is what they want
answers
is for what they long
while nothing can really move them
nothing will shake their stubbornness

maybe the bridge has to collapse first
and fall down upon their heads
because the walls they run into
seem not hard enough.

SATISFACTION

We crave for satisfaction
while losing ourselves
in the process
chasing those endless ambitions.

THE PLANET

Some people want to save the planet
while destroying themselves.

How does that work?

NEW TREES

For new trees to grow
we have to water the seeds.

We are the seed.

NOURISH

We have to first be nourished within
before we can nourish the world.

REMEMBER

Seek and you will find, seek and you will find. Seek not within your mind, but listen to your heart. All answers are hidden in the depths of your Self. Believe in them, believe in what you feel. Feeling is truth, feeling is real.
Thinking is vague, thinking is unreliable. One moment you think this, the other moment you change. The voice within tells you all that you need. Listen to it, even if you don't know how. Listen to your heart, just do it right now.
Right there; that is the place. Remember this moment, and do it every day. You have the answers, you have the solutions. Don't wait for them to come from outside, because those are merely illusions, creating confusion. Truth is within, and not outside of yourself. You knew this already, but now it was time to remember it. Remember your Self.

EDUCATE

Educate yourself
Listen to your heart.

DON'T THINK

I don't really think
I feel what I say
it sprouts in my heart
then flows to my brain
the channel is made
that is the link
now I see clear
I don't even blink
I love what I feel
I love what I say
what do you feel?
can you relate?

TRUE LOVE

True love is an eternal being
beyond limits and boundaries;
it just is.

It is the love you feel
without even knowing the person.
It is the type of love which fills your cup
and makes you feel absolutely satisfied with your self,
your environment,
and life.

Drink from its source.

Here.

LOVE IS

You cannot first be in love
to then suddenly be out of love
that is not possible
love is love
love will always remain love.
Either you loved someone for the wrong reasons
for your own needs
or you didn't love them at all.

Love is.

RELATIONSHIPS

A strong and balanced relationship between two partners is the foundation of society as a whole. It is the representation of two people willing to unite and grow collectively, while never forgetting the importance of Self-discovery and spiritual growth. It is an act of devotion towards yourself, each other and life. It's a divine play which reflects the authentic love we all hold within our hearts.

If the balance is respected and both persons are equally willing to support those values, it can become a beautiful manifestation of joy, happiness and truth.

This is what we are destined to experience within our relationships, but often we tend to look for quick romance, sensation and excitement; while this only leads us further away from the deep peace we are all yearning for.

FRAGRANT

She became as fragrant
as a flower
from the moment
she valued
her own beauty.

SHE

She walked the earth
with a sense of gratitude
a sense of freedom
the world had never seen
as if she felt
she knew
and understood
that her innocence
was all the time
protecting her.

JEALOUSY

Feeling jealous about someone else is a destructive habit that kills our inner joy and satisfaction. This competitive mentality only generates fear and doubts in our minds, while it prevents our individual creativity to blossom.
We should try to look at others as a source of inspiration, in order to discover and manifest our own potential. By doing so, we will not only learn from each other, but also enjoy the connection we share.

A CHOICE

I had to face hate
to learn how to love.

Now I can choose.

BECOME

The mind is a powerful place. It makes you believe
it is in charge, but it's not. It is merely a tool for
you to remember yourself. Those memories are
vague. Often you recall, but you don't pay attention
to them.
The mind is a powerful place. It makes you feel
lost, but you're not. You are a source of love, a
bundle of joy, which the mind cannot fully
apprehend. It has to be felt inside, in every fiber of
your being. You cannot analyse it, neither control.
First, you have to become that pure Self that lives
in your heart. Eventually, the mind will enjoy.

CAGE

The cage is the mind
the soul is the bird
the door is the heart
the key is the door.

THE KEY

The key to your heart
lies hidden between the silence
of your thoughts

the key to your heart
lies in seeing all beauty around you
which cannot be bought

the key to your heart
is to choose love and humility
over arrogance and pain

the key to your heart
is the only way
to release the bird from its cage

the key to your heart
makes you become one
with your true nature

eternity and faith.

TASTE

The freedom of choice is beautiful
it is the most precious gift one has ever received
to love or to hate
to give or to take
to share or to conquer
to do or to wonder

it's all just a matter of taste.

WHEN A CHILD CRIES

When a child cries
you have to feel what to do
you can't just react
like a superior fool
do you feel?
and understand the situation
do you love?
and give time for contemplation

when a child cries
the best you can do
is to stop thinking for a while
and just become you.

STRESS

They are shouting
I'm in bed
they are screaming
I can't rest
stress
is what turns love into hate
stress
turns differences into a debate
debates leading nowhere
only more stress

it's like a disease
a parasite
dividing each other
it is the biggest distraction
to love one another
stress
starts in the body
conquers the mind
only one thing can free us
the heart
seek   and you will find.

CHILDREN

If children learn that winning is important
everything else makes them feel like a loser.

SCHOOL

When school was finished
I finally had time to study

life.

117

INNOCENCE

Innocence lost
the world is in trouble
innocence lost
the world is a jungle
the world is a maze
it's a magical web
it leads you to nothing
it plays with your head
it tells you to want
much more than you need
it tells you to lust
it tells you to greed
it breathes in your neck
it leads you astray
it gives you no answers
it shows you no way

innocence won
the world is no longer
innocence won
the world lost its power
innocence won
the world is the same
innocence won
within you have changed.

GRAVITY

Being able
to resist the pressure
of others
is a sign
of gravity
and strength.

DRAMA

People are attracted to drama
it's like an addiction
that's what the world taught us
to embrace all of our misery
as if it is some kind of a victory
pathetic
this will lead us nowhere
but only more drama
check yourself
if you truly want to live
open your eyes
and look for options
look for solutions
for answers
because they will come
because life supports you
the world doesn't.

REALISE

When you will realise
that anything which is untruth
does not give you any satisfaction
you will beg for truth
and truth will come.

WATCH

A solution could be
to just watch
like a bird in a tree
beyond judgements or expectations
just to see
to see what happens
when you don't judge or engage
maybe it restores the balance
maybe this is the way.

MANTRA

Doing something that makes
your heart feel good
your mind at rest
and your soul at ease
is the most powerful mantra in life.

FORGIVENESS

Forgiveness is the greatest tool
of the human brain
if you don't use it
you're only hurting yourself
no one else cares.

AWARENESS

Everything starts with awareness
that is why I'm spreading it
for you to become aware of your own Self
to become aware of life and everything around you.

Without awareness we remain ignorant
like an uneducated child
awareness will broaden your options
it will open your mind.

The next step is to do something with it
to actually manifest this awareness in your own being
to connect your mental awareness with your inner voice
so they can become one
and you will become one.

Life will be much easier
and enjoyable
trust me
life will be fun.

GHOSTWRITER

I have a ghostwriter
my heart
it tells my mind what to write
it's quite easy
I just have to listen.

THE BOAT

There is an unlimited source of inspiration
flowing from the depths of my heart
protected by a firm boat floating on endless waters
no waves can disturb it
no storm can change its course
the ship has everything under control
my heart is its captain
the boat is my soul.

PEN

This pen in my hand
will never run dry
it will never stop writing
it can never sink
because the content of its soul
is filled with ink.

I WOULD

If I could talk to you in person
I would write you a poem.

REVELATION

The revelation is near
the people are ready
they are prepared
hungry and thirsty

the answer is here
the moment is now
the solution is you
you wonder how

you are the power
you are the love
you are the channel
for God up above

you are the light
open your heart
you are the change
right from the start

freedom is here
have courage and trust
look deep in yourself
the answer is us

it's in our own soul
has always been
and now is the time
for it to be seen

listen to it
and shine like a star
the revelation is here:
become who you are.

ALL

From nothing
everything came
every atom
every plane
nothing was there
now it has heart
now it can feel
now it can see
nothing was there
now it is free.

From nothing we come
to nothing we go
now nothing is all
it's calling our soul.

THE ENERGY

The energy rises in abundance
when you allow it to whisper and flow
the second you feel you're in charge
is the moment you're losing control
the energy works on its own
using you to radiate all of its light
the energy can't be contained
it is neither dead, asleep or alive
the energy is all
there was
there is
and will be
the energy is inside
within you
within them
and in me.

WARRIOR

Silence is the way of the warrior
practicing amidst rumors at night
righteousness— his ultimate goal
and the battle for he is willing to fight.

Truth is his armor
love for the people gives him powers to fly
he fights for justice beyond karma
and for that, he is willing to die.

"Stand tall!"
he commands his brothers and sisters,
"Behold proudly the walls of your heart!
don't ever let them be broken
for once they are shattered
life becomes utterly dark.

Have faith and courage in life
for its ways will make you come clean
once you surrender the strive
to become powerful, angry, and mean.

Open your eyes for all people
and see them as kins of your tribe
choose the path of love over evil
and one day, the whole world will unite!"

SEE

I see things
as they are.

What do you see?

DISCOVER

Do you see what I can see?
can you feel what I can feel?
a pleasant world
in a state of bliss
free for all mankind
a caring world
full of forgiveness
wherein temptations
are no longer disturbing our minds
a beautiful place
of harmony, justice, equality and love
an ultimate revelation
wherein liberation finally falls down upon us
an overwhelming happening
that transforms us deeply within
an absolute destination
to rise above our own misidentifications and sins
to free us all
from destruction and all our illusions
to finally see clear
that we have to look within for all our solutions

sleep further
dear mind
and you will eternally fall
wake now
dear soul
and you will conquer it all

how to find
this magical place
full of joy, happiness and truth

ask only your Self
truthfully
and one day
you will discover your fountain of youth.

TOGETHER

Rise up
dear brothers and sisters
it is time to fight for the truth
we have been lied to since childhood
and during all the days of our youth
they tell us to seek money
to yearn for status, recognition and power
but isn't that too artificial to be valued as good?
how can this nourish our body?
our Soul?
our whole being?
it doesn't taste at all like the most nourishing food
our thirst for love can never be quenched
when we follow those worldly possessions in vain
love is the only food for our Spirit
while everything else causes hatred and pain
they don't teach us about sharing, compassion or
purpose
they only want us to follow their ways
but the paths they walk are destructive
while they try to seduce us every day
stop
look deep down yourself
and discover
the powers and truth you behold
for the knowledge and wisdom within
is much more worth than anything you have ever been
told

I see you
my brothers and sisters
my relatives, my companions and friends
together we shall rise
grow and discover
together we'll walk
together— we'll win.

THE VOICE

When the voice of the heart is calling you
reaching out for you to embrace yourself
you better listen
you better pay attention
as its screams might one day fade
together with all the broken dreams
you saw slowly drifting away.

If this intense sense of this heart can be manifested through these words, then please let them open your doors. Let the desire that supports them enter your being and awaken that tremendous potential of love you are holding inside. Let them grasp those deepest feelings you are hiding within and pull them out so that you can share them with the world around you.

What else can be possibly done to enlighten your soul with the light that can illuminate the whole world? What more can be done for you to unlock that majestic presence of truth that lingers deep in your heart?

Can you not see that everything that we have ever invented, created, or manifested, came from that beautiful place inside our own Self?

Open yourself up to it. Listen to that place that comforts you in times of complete desperation. Talk with its presence. And manifest its wishes.

RECONCILE

What we need to do right now
is to sit down and meditate
reconcile the way we have lived
and forgive all our mistakes
forgive also those around you
as the past is no more
use all of its struggles and misery
to dig deep down your own core
to become one with your Self
and the way that you feel
to feel what you are
and let your truth be revealed
unlock your powers
the potential and talents you got
open your heart
because that's where it all starts.

KNOCK KNOCK

We create
a thousand ways
to distract ourselves
but sooner or later
confrontation
shall come knocking
at our doors.

Always remember that you are never alone in this world. That you are all the time supported by a deeper source living in the depths of your heart. A beautiful source connecting all human beings beyond race, gender, culture, or age. A source that manifests that pure love within, which we all turn to in times of need and despair. A type of love that rises beyond our mental expectations and judgements. It's just there at those exact same moments when we need it the most.

This is the love we should value and try to manifest in our daily lives. This is the love that will truly nourish our being. This is the beauty of life.

It takes courage and faith to accept it; to embrace it. Because we are taught to believe in a dependent type of love, which mainly focuses on satiating our own needs and desires. An artificial type of love that only feeds our ego. This is a very primitive love that never lasts and only leads us into illusions.

Free yourself and love your heart. Because your heart is detached. It is absolutely free. Because your heart loves you; and everyone else on the planet.

THE SPIRIT

In our heart resides the Spirit
an eternal reflection of light
it's just there
watching
as a witness
whatever happens in life.

Its power is unlimited
its source has neither beginning nor end
it provides us with wisdom, compassion, and truth
as well as understanding, forgiveness, and strength.

It liberates us from bondage
from our wicked opinions and thoughts
it opens new doors and options
for us as people
as humanity
to rejoice in its blessings of love.

THE CURE

If I could write a cure for humanity
I would title it: "love"

the purest form of love
flowing from heart to heart
beyond our mental limitations

a divine source of love
boosting our immune systems
saving this creation

a healing type of love
enlightening the soul of the world
bringing us all in harmony

an absolute connection
with our deepest Self and each other
manifesting togetherness, wisdom and reality

a final revelation
to discover our Spirit
deep within our hearts

a complete resurrection
feeding our roots
back to where it starts

this is all I want to write about
this is all I want to feel
this is all I truly care about
because it feels so real

if only we would access it
if only we would care
if only we would manifest
the love that we can share.

JOURNEY

We are all on a journey
towards the best version of ourselves
sometimes we get distracted
sometimes we get confused
but deep down we all yearn for truth
for food
food for our soul
that's why we live
that's why we grow
sometimes we're lost
but then we get reminded in times of struggle or need
our worst feelings are our greatest teacher
but often we tend to repeat
repeat over and over again
like a drama
without end
to eventually be reminded again
and again.

I remind myself daily
through meditation
that is my way
it is my guide and my direction
it is my freedom
it is my faith.

My reminder of Self and manifestation of love
comes through meditation
silently being aware of everything around me
just to watch
it's beautiful
I wish you could see.

I follow the technique of Sahaja Yoga
the union of the Self with its own source
it's completely free
feel free to try it
and open your own doors.

WITNESS

Looking at the world as a witness
without judgements or expectations
through thoughtless awareness
is the natural state of being
you truly wish to be.

When we are having negative emotions, it doesn't mean that we have to identify with them. Sometimes they come unexpectedly without any specific cause or reason. A good way to deal with emotions of doubt, fear or insecurity, is to watch them as an observant. As if they are entities on their own which are just trying to trouble you. You can watch them from your deeper Self and connect with who you truly are within. By doing so, these emotions will never get the chance to dominate you, while your inner gravity will make them fade away spontaneously.

It is a form of healing wherein you overcome your problems from within, by becoming a witness. You just have to practice it, and eventually it will happen by itself. Meditation can help you with that.

INCOMPARABLE

The love
we can discover
within our own being
is incomparable
with the love
we can ever receive
from anyone else.

WALK WITH ME

Walk with me
so we can rejoice
in the heart of the universe.

CONTENTS